STUCK TOAST
AND
MUD PIES

Poems for Kids
by
June Estep Fiorelli

Ordering Information:
To order additional copies, or inquire about bulk orders for schools or other groups, please visit:
http://www.JuneEstepFiorelli.com

Book design by Eric Sheridan Wyatt, for Words Matter:
http://www.WordsMatterESW.com/stucktoast

ISBN: 978-1-312-32118-2

With love to my dear daughter, Ann Lawson
Fiorelli, who saved my life...more than once;
and,
To her husband, Richard A. Croley, Ph.D.
who faithfully read his Weekly Reader and
remembers every word.

ALSO BY JUNE ESTEP FIORELLI

BIOGRAPHY

Fannie Lou Hamer: A Voice for Freedom
Young Adult Series   Avisson Press, Greensboro, NC

OTHER PUBLICATIONS

Hopscotch for Girls
    Rainbows (To See A Rainbow) p.58
    The Questionmark Twins p.95
    Stuck Toast   p. 57

Boys' Quest
    Good Old Gravity p.59

Nick Jr.
    Noodle Section of Nick Jr.
    Nick Jr. Family Magazine

Teaching and Learning Company
    Teaching and Learning Magazine
    Teaching and Learning Book

Wild Outdoor World Magazine
    "No Such Thing as a Seagull"

SIRS Discoverer CD-ROM
    "No Such Thing as a Seagull"

Waterford Institute
    Big Words About Me From A to Z

AWARDS

Stuck Toast; The Questionmark Twins; The Teacher Always Picks on Me; The Remarkable Bubbles of Mary Lee Hubbles; Announcement: Social Studies Test Today.

TABLE OF CONTENTS

WET FEET AND OTHER SOGGY STUFF

MOM FIBBED?

I heard the rain all through the night.
It pounded on the roof.
Mom told me something strange today.
I looked outside for proof.
The puddles made a bathtub
For some birds and hopping frogs.
So, why did my mom tell me
It was raining cats and dogs?

STORM

Racing bolts of
Lightning flashing.
Boomda! Boomda!
Thunder crashing.
Rain is streaking.
Winds are reeling.
Storms give me
A scary feeling.

I'm protecting
My dog, Rover.
We'll be glad
When this is over.

GRANDMA'S UMBRELLA

My grandma calls umbrellas
By a very silly name.
She opens up her bumbershoot.
When it begins to rain.
Her bumbershoot is purple,
And when it's a rainy day
We both hold on together
So it doesn't blow away.
The crowds may push, the wind may howl
The cars and taxis toot,
But we stay dry and cozy
Under grandma's bumbershoot.

PUDDLE MIRRORS

I gaze in a puddle
And what do I see?
A bright cloudless sky
That's as blue as can be,
A face filled with freckles,
Eyes green as the sea,
And the long twisted braids
Of red-headed me.

Stuck Toast and Mud Pies

MADE IT!

Plink! Plink!
Home I dash,
Duck the raindrops
Dodge a splash.
Leap up steps
And rush inside
Before the heavens
Open wide.

STUCK INSIDE

I couldn't play outside all week,
The weather's been so bad.
I'm tired of all the rain and sleet,
To ride my bike would be a treat.
The sun would make my day complete,
I want dry ground beneath my feet.
Instead, I'm staying in the house
AGAIN! And feeling mad.

THIRSTY PANSIES

The welcome rain is falling
On the pansies in my yard.
They've turned their wilted petals up,
They're trying really hard
To lift their eager faces high
And drink the raindrops in
So they can change what seemed a frown
Into a happy grin.

SPRING RAIN

I lift my face into the gentle rain
And breathe in deeply.
The world smells new today.
Flower smells…
Warm earthen smells…
Fresh morning breeze smells.
Rain…spring cleaning our world.

WHERE THE RAIN GOES

Rain is falling all about,
On the roof and through the spout.
Swooshing out into the lane,
Down the street, into the drain,
Joining rivers, running free,
Rushing out to meet the sea.

RAINBOWS ON HIGH

Whenever sun is shining through a misty rain
I rush outside and, gazing way up high,
I see, with every color in my crayon box,
A rainbow sweeping wide across the sky.

GOOD NIGHT, GOOD NIGHT

The sun wakes up in the eastern sky
And hour by hour it rides up high
Then sinks toward the west and dips its head
Into the ocean and goes to bed.

Stuck Toast and Mud Pies

UMBRELLAS ON PARADE

From my apartment way up high
I watch umbrella tops pass by.

Some small, some big, some in between,
Some striped or flowered, pink or green.

Some bounce and bob, some twirl about,
Some dart and dodge, weave in and out.

Some see a door and duck inside.
Some board a bus and catch a ride.

One hails a cab, and in it hops.
Then suddenly the downpour stops.

The sky turns clear and here's the sun!
Umbrellas snap shut, one by one.

NEW BOOTS

Splish, splash, splish, splash,
I'm on my way to school.
I jump in every puddle...SPLAT!
Muddy, wet, and cool.

I slosh through all the gutters
Where the water's running high,
Checking if my new rain boots
Will keep me nice and dry.

RAIN AT NIGHT

Drip, drip, Drop, drop.
Listening for the rain to stop.
Covers pulled up to my nose.
Warm and cozy, head to toes.

Outside, animals abound;
Each one with its nighttime sound.
Will they find a place to hide
Soft and dry as mine inside?

If only I could share my bed
With every creature sleepy-head.
Drip, drip, Drop, drop.
Wishing that the rain would stop.

Stuck Toast and Mud Pies

NO "SNOW DAY" TODAY

The snow fell softly through the night.
The world outside is dazzling white.

As far away as I can see
Snow's blanketed each fence, each tree.

I turn the news on. Will they say,
"The storm was bad. No school today?"

I dream of sledding with my friend.
We'll build a fort and play pretend.

What's that? The plow has cleared our road?
The sand truck followed with its load?

I hear the school bus give three toots.
I pull on coat and scarf and boots.

My hopes for playing in the snow
Are gone, and off to school I go.

ICE STORM

Tic, Tic...Ping, Ping
Icy crystals strike against the windowpane.
The view outside becomes a shadow world
Through windows glazed with drops of frozen rain.

THE CAT-O'-NINE-TAIL

The cat-o'-nine-tail loves wet feet.
It thinks a marsh is really neat.
It doesn't wheeze or sneeze ah-choo,
It never needs a shot for flu
Or ever get a runny nose
From being damp about the toes.

And even though the polliwogs,
The slimy eels and warty frogs
And minnows swim among its roots,
It simply won't wear rubber boots!

Yet we, in spite of hats and coats,
And scarves wound tightly round our throats,
Get colds and coughs and go to bed
With fever and an achy head.

"Now, is it fair," we ask in vain,
"That you survive out in the rain?"

The cat-o'-nine does not respond.
It finds life perfect in the pond.

Stuck Toast and Mud Pies

DRIVING HOME

It's late at night
We're in our car.
We're driving home,
It's very far.

A storm whips up
Tree branches snap.
The windshield wipers
Softly slap.

The storm grows wilder
As we ride,
But we are quiet
Here inside.

The motor purrs,
The wipers sweep.
Their steady beat
Puts me to sleep.

SCHOOL RHYMES ROCK

SPITBALLS

I wait till Teacher
Turns her back,
Wet a spitball
Aim it...Whack!
Sticks on Rudy's
Slicked down hair.
He doesn't even
Know it's there.
The kids all giggle,
Pointing to it.
I act cool
Like I didn't do it.

Teacher turns,
She points at me!
How did she know?
How could she see?

I guess it's true
Just as she said.
She has two eyes
In the back of her head.

MATH PROBLEMS

ADDITION DILEMMA

One boy has ten books,
Another has twelve.
Please write down the total amount.

I start adding up
But then I get stuck.
I've run out of fingers to count.

MODERN "TIMES"

I spent the whole year in grade three
Reciting TABLES endlessly.

I learned to say them, one through four
Then couldn't memorize one more.

In fourth and fifth I really tried
So hard, I think my brain had fried.

But in grade six the teacher knew
Exactly what I had to do.

Now TABLES cause me no more strife.
The calculator saved my life.

Stuck Toast and Mud Pies

SHORT DIVISION PROBLEM

You call and order pizza
That's been cut in nine large slices.
You cut each slice in half again
With one of those devices.
If six of you are sharing it
You get how many slices?

We just get three? The answer is
A pepperoni crisis!

RABBITS CAN'T SUBTRACT

A farm owned by Jones now has three thousand rabbits.
Bill's farm has two hundred and four.
Tell which has the most. Next tell how you must solve it.
Then write down just how many more.

It's clear that the Jones farm has many more rabbits.
I have to subtract and to borrow.
The answer today is two, seven nine six—but
That won't be correct by tomorrow.

THE SAD EXCUSE CHART

The Sad Excuse Chart hangs up front.
My name is listed there.
I meant to do my homework, so
It really isn't fair.

I had to take the garbage out.
Dad made me mow the lawn.
I stayed up late and did my math...
This morning it was gone.

My uncle came from Cleveland, and
He took us out to eat.
I threw up twice when I got home.
Mom said it was the heat.

My brother kicked a soccer ball,
I ducked, but still got hit.
My mother went out shopping, so
I had to baby-sit.

I had to get a haircut, 'cause
My mom and dad insisted,
So I didn't do my language arts
And now my name is listed.

My little sister pestered me.
The TV blared all night.
I sprained my wrist at baseball, and
It hurt too much to write.

I told my teacher all my woes.
It wasn't any use.
He rolled his eyes and checked my name;
Another "sad excuse."

MY FAVORITE SUBJECT

I like Bus
And Art is fun.
Math's okay
When class is done.

I like Lunch
And I like Hall,
But I like Recess
Best of all.

FIRST IN LINE

I push ahead. I'm first in line
When we go out to play
So I can grab the bat and ball
And choose the teams MY way.

At plays I want to have a view
Not blocked by someone's head.
I leave the middle row, and grab
An aisle seat instead.

On school trips when we take the bus
It pays to have MY knack
Of pushing, so I'm first on board
To claim the seat in back.

"New rules for recess," Teacher says.
I shove up front—I win.
She looks right in my eyes, and adds,
"You pushed, so you stay in!"

Stuck Toast and Mud Pies

ALPHABETICAL SEATING

My parents named me Aaron,
And although I'm not a runt,
My name begins with double A
So I must sit up front.

If goof-off kids don't know the page
They simply scrunch down low.
I have to know the answers, 'cause
There's nowhere I can go.

I can't send notes, I dare not talk,
I always clean the board.
I pass out papers, but just once—
I'd like to be ignored.

I cannot sneak a little snack,
And when we have a quiz
I cannot peek at notes I took…
I have to be a whiz.

Before next year I'll change my name
To William, Zane, or Zack.
That way I'll finally get my chance
To sit way down in back.

THE TEACHER ALWAYS PICKS ON ME

My teacher always picks on me.
He never picks on others.
He lets them get away with things.
He never calls THEIR mothers.

"Please sit up straight," he sternly says.
"Don't slouch down in your seat.
Your hair's too spiked; you talk too much;
Your homework's incomplete."

"Stop sending notes," he orders me.
"You're here in school to learn.
Don't shove your way into the line;
You need to wait your turn."

"Stay in and clean your desk," he scolds.
I thought it looked okay.
Alphonzo's is a total mess
But he goes out to play.

I saw Jolene send notes to Don.
I heard Patricia swear.
When other kids do things like that
Why isn't Teacher there?

Now, I'm not any angel, and
My work may not be best,
But why didn't Teacher notice when
Kim cheated on the test?

When other kids are bad in school
They get away scot-free.
My teacher really is unfair...
He only picks...he always picks...he picks and picks on me!

NEW KID IN SCHOOL

If I hold back the tears,
And I wait just a while,
Maybe someone will speak to me,
Give me a smile.

It's so tough to be new.
It's so hard to know when
Someone nice will say, "Hi!"
And I'll make friends again.

COMPUTER GENERATION

My parents always criticize
If I get C's on quizzes.
But now I've learned computers, and
My folks are not such whizzes.

"Teach us to use the Net," they beg.
I grin. The table's turning.
It's I who am the smart one now
While THEY are slow at learning.

THE LAST ONE PICKED

They choose up teams, last picked is me.
I always strike out one, two, three.

With bases full they call my name.
If we lose now I'll be to blame.

If I don't help someone to score
They'll never pick me anymore.

I start to sweat, I start to drip.
I tell myself to get a grip.

My shoulder's stiff, my forehead burns,
My knees go weak, my stomach churns.

I take my stance, I tremble, shake.
Please let me hit...give me a break.

The pitcher winds, the ball is thrown.
I fan the air...my teammates groan.

A second strike, but then I hit!
The fielder drops it from his mitt!

My team's ahead, we've scored a run.
Is that why kids think baseball's fun?

If that's called fun, I disagree.
For last ones picked, it's agony.

Stuck Toast and Mud Pies

LEARN TO SHARE

The teacher says that we must share
With other kids. It shows we care.

Because we're ladies, gentlemen
We should share paper, pencil, pen.

We share our lunch, we share our snack
We share a treat, we get one back.

We share the chance to choose up sides.
We share the jungle gyms and slides.

We share the field, we share the swing.
We share the cupcakes mothers bring.

We share the bat, we share the ball.
We're told that we must share it all.

So why, if we must share the rest,
We can't share answers on a test?

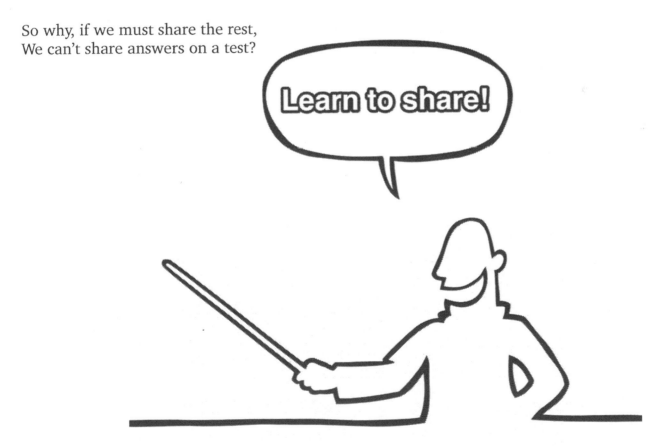

GET IT TOGETHER ... PLEASE

Mom placed my key and lunchbox
On the counter by the door.
But I slept late—it was my fate—
To leave them home once more.

I left my book bag on the bus.
I lost my gloves as well.
I looked around and never found them
Then I heard the bell.

I cannot find my pencil
And my pen is missing, too.
I'm in a bind 'cause I can't find
My homework. What to do?

My teacher, Mom and Dad agree
(They act like they're so wise.)
I can't imagine why they think
I need to organize!

Stuck Toast and Mud Pies

CLASS TRIP

The bus pulls up and on we dart.
We leave for the Museum of Art.
It's not like school when we're away.
It's going to be a fun-filled day.

We push the windows down and wave.
The driver scolds, "Now, you behave!
We're in the middle part of town.
Stay in your seats and settle down!"

Once we arrive, "Take notes," we're told.
I write: *The guards look very old.*
The tour guide yelled. Her voice was loud.
"Don't touch the art. It's not allowed."

Some paintings are extremely small.
Some others fill an entire wall.
The gift shop has neat toys and such.
The trouble is, they charge too much.

We board our bus and head for school.
We sing, we yell, break every rule.
We throw some spitballs, chew some gum.
When Teacher glares we just act dumb.

What did you say? The teacher spoke?
You must be telling me a joke.
A test on what we learned today?
I check my notes. Uh oh, no way.

Impressionism? What is that?
What's pointillism? Who's Cassatt?
We have to know about van Gogh?
And Claude Monet? My notes don't say.

The trip was fun but, as you've guessed,
There's not a chance I'll pass that test!

SO...WHO'S THE NERD?

I always get to class on time,
My homework's always done.
I get straight A's
        In math each day.
I think division's fun.

        The kids don't pick me for their team...
        I seldom kick the ball.
        But I do best
                On every test,
        So, I don't care at all.

They call me "nerd," or so I've heard,
But someday we'll compare
How they'll be known
        When we're all grown
And I'm a millionaire.

Stuck Toast and Mud Pies

FIRST LOVES

DELAYED PROPOSAL

I love a girl...her name's Maureen,
She has red hair; her eyes are green.
Her laugh is bubbly like soda pop,
It makes my heart go flippity-flop.
She flirts with me. I think she knows
How I love the freckles across her nose.
I'd ask her to marry, but I'm afraid.
Maybe next year—when we're in sixth grade.

A SHORT ROMANCE

Matthew's so cute, adorable, smart.
He tells me he likes me. He's won my heart.
But I wish I could shrink and be just a bit smaller
And that he'd start to grow and be six inches taller.
I gaze down at him, and he looks up at me
Which causes the problem between us, you see.
If ever I'm brave and I lean down to kiss him
He's so very short
      I will
          probably
               miss
                   him!

I LOVE SCHOOL

The classroom is the place for me;
I can't think where I'd rather be.
I need the challenge, want it now.
If I can't do it, I learn how.

Assignments are not hard enough.
I beg my teacher, "Make it tough.
More science, more geography,
More grammar, more geometry,
More projects, more reports to write
I'll work on them till late at night."

I've finished every Nancy Drew,
O'Henry, Bloome, Jane Austen, too.
I've practiced how to paraphrase
And read a dozen Shakespeare plays.
I've memorized the poems of Poe,
Of Frost and Whitman, and I know
World leaders, kings and presidents,
And all of their accomplishments.
On maps I locate Paraguay,
Thailand, Shanghai and Uruguay.

Though classmates might prefer to goof,
I hate vacations, that's the truth.
I know some friends think I'm a fool.
I'm not. I'm smart. I just love school.

Stuck Toast and Mud Pies

REPORT CARDS TODAY

My class is all up tight because today's report card day.
But I stay cool; I'm no one's fool. I know what mine will say.

My father's an accountant so he knows how to compute.
But unlike Dad, I barely add, while he can do square root.

My mother knows the dates of wars. She teaches history.
But every bit, I must admit, is simply Greek to me.

My grandpa did experiments with microbes, germs and stuff.
But there's no way I'll get an A in science. It's too tough.

My grandma was an editor. She checked what writers wrote.
But I regret I still don't get the way to write a quote.

Why can't I learn where commas go? Recite the kings and queens?
Experiment? And do percent? It should be in my genes.

It's strange I am so different. My brain is really wild.
Was I adopted? Maybe dropped when I was just a child?

My parents see my card. "An A in Art!" they proudly say.
"Your oils and drawings are so good; they'll hang in the Met one day."

BARF TIME

Our teacher pulled a big surprise...
A test in history.
I haven't read the chapter so
There's just one hope for me.

I go to Teacher's desk and groan.
"I have to see the nurse.
My stomach hurts; I might throw up;
My headache's getting worse."

The nurse first takes my temperature.
She has me rest awhile.
A half hour later I feel fine.
I go back with a smile.

"I'm glad you're feeling better now,"
The teacher says. "I knew
You'd get well soon, so I delayed
The test time just for you."

Stuck Toast and Mud Pies

THE PERFECT SEATING PLAN

Teacher, I don't want to sit next to Pete.
He steals my homework and tries to cheat.

   Teacher, I don't want to sit next to Rose.
   She bites her nails and she picks her nose.

      Teacher, I don't want to sit next to Lee.
      He sends me notes and he flirts with me.

         Teacher, I don't want to sit next to Jack.
         He burps a lot and he steals my snack.

Teacher, I don't want to sit next to Claire.
Her hair has cooties. I saw them there.

   Teacher, I don't want to sit next to Joe.
   His neck is dirty. He has B.O.

      Teacher, I don't want to sit next to Tad.
      He coughs all day and his breath smells bad.

         Teacher, you say I must sit next to Mike?
         Oh wow! What luck! He's the boy I like!

BULLY, BULLY

Bully, Bully,
Steals my lunch.
Gives my arm
A rabbit punch.

Breaks my pencil
On the sly.
Loves to make
The small kids cry.

He teases me
About my clothes.
I feel like bloodying
His nose.

But I hold back
Because I know
He's sad. The teacher
Told us so.

He bullies us
But in the end—
What he wants most
Is just a friend.

Stuck Toast and Mud Pies

SHOULDA, WOULDA, COULDA

I shoulda, woulda, coulda
Studied hard and gotten A,
But I didn't.

I shoulda, woulda, coulda
Done my homework - gotten C,
But I didn't.

I shoulda, woulda, coulda
Spent less time at the TV,
But I didn't.

I shoulda, woulda, coulda
Made an effort - gotten D,
But I didn't.

They shoulda, woulda, coulda
At least promoted me,
But they didn't!

PIZZA TODAY

I saw Mom pack my lunch,
But I thought, There's no way
I'll eat stuff made at home
When the school lunch today's
Yummy PIZZA!

I had visions of cheese
Melting bubbly and thick.
They give seconds to those
Who have wolfed theirs down quick.
Double PIZZA!

So, I sorta made out
That I kinda forgot.
Left my brown bag at home
I'd eat lunch steamy hot
Spicy PIZZA!

Now, it's just before lunch.
One guess, who should appear?
But my mom, with a smile,
Saying, "Here's your lunch, dear."
Bye, bye, PIZZA!

Stuck Toast and Mud Pies

ANNOUNCEMENT:
SOCIAL STUDIES TEST TODAY

ALL THIS YEAR:

In Social Studies, which I hate,
I cannot seem to concentrate.
My study skills are second rate.
I watch TV, procrastinate.

ALL THIS WEEK:

The teacher took time to relate
The knowledge we must demonstrate:
The thirteen colonies and the date
When each of them became a state;
The traitor, Arnold, and his fate;
What steps it takes to legislate,
To immigrate, to emigrate.

The Lincoln-Douglas great debate;
When Lincoln said, "Emancipate;"
How to become a candidate;
The date when we inaugurate;
The break in at the Watergate;
The order to desegregate.

NIGHT BEFORE THE TEST:

My memory is not so great.
My brain starts to evaporate.
My favorite show is on at eight,
I'm sure the studying can wait.

IT'S TEST DAY:

Uh oh, I'll have to guess-ta-mate.
My grade? I hate to contemplate.
I should have studied. It's too late.
I only hope I graduate!

SCHOOL'S OUT

Last day of school...
I feel elated.
In spite of Cs
On tests I hated
The teacher says
I graduated!

Hurray!

Stuck Toast and Mud Pies

FESTIVITIES AND FUN

Stuck Toast and Mud Pies

A VALENTINE PROMISE

February 14

I'll wash the dishes one whole week.
I'll clean my room. I'll make my bed.
I'll draw a special card for you
With colored hearts of brightest red.

I'll circle them with daffodils
Then add a cooing turtledove.
I'll write your names across the top
To let you know it's you I love.

Dear Mom and Dad, I'm glad you're mine;
So, may I be your valentine?

Celebrating the Fourth

July 4

I love our country's quiet farms, its hills, its open space;
Our cities flashing neon lights, their noise, their frantic pace.
I love our fertile soil, the trees, the mountains' mighty lift;
The power from our falls and streams, each one a precious gift.
I love the caring people who protect our living earth,
Conserving air and water, and respecting what they're worth.

I love the courage of our forebears crossing wind-blown seas
To find a place to make a home; to worship as they please.
I love the brave from far away who came, and from the start
Enriched our country, made it strong, with hand and mind and heart.

I love the early settlers, the hard battles that they fought
To break the rule of tyrants; win the justice that they sought.
I love the Declaration, graceful words that guarantee
Our right to live as equals, to be happy, and be free.

I love parades that mark the day, the stars and stripes held high,
Its red and white and blue ablaze against a cloudless sky.
I love the festive floats, the squads of soldiers and cadets,
The blaring bands, the drums, the baton-twirling majorettes.

I love when darkness falls and there's excitement in the air;
When pyrotechnic colors wrap me in their blinding glare.
I love the thrill I'm feeling, and I'm proud we found this way
To celebrate the land I love on Independence Day.

THE SPOOKY SOUNDS OF HALLOWEEN

October 31

On Halloween we must be brave
When skeletons rise from the grave.
Their dry bones clatter in the breeze
As moaning winds blow through the trees.

Black cats hump up their backs and yowl.
The zombies stomp; the banshees howl.
The ravens screech their raucous, "Caw!"
While perched on scarecrows stuffed with straw.

A witch streaks wide across the skies.
She cackles madly as she flies.
A werewolf growls and bares his fangs.
A vampire groans, a shutter bangs.

In haunted houses squeaky doors,
Fat rats that scratch, and creaky floors,
The rattling chains and ghostly sighs
Make spines go tingle, goose bumps rise.

Some think these spooky sounds are neat,
But me...I'm glad there's trick or treat.

Stuck Toast and Mud Pies

THE DAY OF THE DEAD Dia de los Muertos

Mexico and Around the World   October 31-November 2

THE HISTORY

About three thousand years ago, the Aztec tribes of Mexico
Held rituals to celebrate their dear ones who had died.
They thought of death as part of life, and felt their loved ones could return.
To greet them, late in harvest time some days were set aside.
With trophy skulls displayed as symbols of both death and then rebirth,
They danced and held a joyous feast to welcome them to earth.

In fifteen twenty-one, Conquistadores from Spain took Aztec lands.
They found the rituals shocking; they'd been taught to mourn the dead.
They tried to ban the Aztecs' ancient pagan rites forevermore;
To force them to accept their solemn view of death instead,
And celebrate on certain dates when Catholic Holy Days occurred:
Allhallows Eve came first, All Saints' Day next, All Souls' Day third.

CELEBRATIONS NOW:

Today not only Mexicans, but folks from all around the globe,
Combine the Christian rituals with those of tribal ways.
They build fine altars, called *ofrendas*, in the graveyards or their homes,
Adorning them with marigolds, and colorful displays
Of fruit and nuts and pumpkin. Then as thoughts of ones they love unfold,
Their photographs are shared and favorite anecdotes are told.

Their festivals, parades and costumes may take many months to plan.
The children choose a decorated chocolate skull to eat.
A bread is baked, called *Pan de Muerto,* only for this one event,
And skeletons of cardboard dance a jig on jointed feet.
Day of the Dead has changed since Aztec times, but joy is still a part
Of honoring the memories of those close to our heart.

YUMMY, YUMMY TURKEY

Thanksgiving: Fourth Thursday in November

Buy the turkey and potatoes,
Put them in the shopping cart.
Add the yams and peas and onions,
Cranberries bright red and tart.

Fill the bird with spicy stuffing,
Put it in to slowly roast.
Make the pies, one mince, one pumpkin,
These are what I love the most.

Lay the cloth upon the table,
Napkins, spoons and forks and knives.
Add some flowers, red and yellow,
Then our family arrives.

Take the turkey from the oven,
Cover it with silver foil.
Mash the turnips and potatoes,
Golden yams begin to boil.

Time to carve the juicy turkey.
Drumsticks are my favorite treat.
We all gather 'round the table,
Giving thanks for what we eat.

Oh, I groan, my stomach's hurting.
There was too much on my plate.
Now I look just like the turkey,
Stuffed with yummy food I ate.

Stuck Toast and Mud Pies

DEAR SANTA

All I want for Christmas

My note to Santa Claus this year
Was written very clearly:
"A puppy's all I really want
And, oh, I want it dearly."

On Christmas morn my spirits sank.
There wasn't any puppy.
Instead, I found beneath the tree,
A fish tank with a guppy.

"Oh, Santa what a big mistake,"
I really felt like yelling.
"How could you mix up P with G?
Are you that bad at spelling?"

I smiled bravely, acted pleased,
But I was only faking.
I fed the fish and watched it swim.
Inside, my heart was breaking.

At noon my gram and gramp arrived,
Their arms held something yapping.
You guessed! A pup with wagging tail
And soft brown ears a-flapping.

I'm sorry poor old Santa had
A problem with my letter.
But I'm so glad he passed it on
To someone who reads better.

WE CELEBRATE CHRISTMAS

A Christian Holy Day and Celebration
December 25

An eastern star led wise men
      To the place where baby Jesus lay.

The shepherds left their flocks
      And gathered round his humble bed of hay.

In manhood, Jesus traveled widely,
      Teaching goodness on His way.

Now, Christians all around the world
      Observe His birth on Christmas Day.

They gather in their churches,
      Sing noels and pray while candles glow.

They brightly decorate their homes
      And hang bright stockings in a row

And trim a fragrant pine with shiny tinsel,
      Ornaments and snow.

They feast and celebrate with gifts
      As did the wise men long ago.

HANUKKAH: THE FESTIVAL OF LIGHTS

A Jewish Celebration
A Time between Late November and Late December

Long, long ago an evil Grecian ruler
Despoiled the holy Temple of the Jews.
Then Judah Maccabee won back the Temple.
For Jewish people, that was joyous news.

To purify the Temple, oil was needed.
How could their small supply burn eight full nights?
But miracle of miracles, the oil lasted,
And so began the Festival of Lights.

Today the families gather 'round menorahs
Which hold nine candles, one of greater height.
Each night it's used to light another candle
Till on the eighth night, all are burning bright.

To celebrate, they dance a merry hora
And spin a top, called dreidel, round and round.
They eat crisp latkas, sing songs of remembrance
Which fill their homes with love and joyous sound.

THE FAST OF RAMADAN

A Muslim Celebration
The Ninth Month of the Islamic Calendar

The Traditions:
Once we, as Muslim children, reach the age of twelve
We join our elders in the Fast of Ramadan.
We neither eat nor drink from dawn to dusk
And go to mosques to read our holy book, Quran.

To start each day before the sun comes up
We eat a meal called suhoor; then begin our fast.
We pray for all the hungry and the poor.
Once dark we eat, but first sweet drinks and dates are passed.

When Ramadan is over, celebrations break our fast.
We wear our finest clothes; adorn our homes with lights.
Gifts are exchanged, and families gather for large feasts.
We feed the poor to share our blessings and delights.

The Meaning:
Long years ago, Muhammad wandered through the desert's barren sands,
Concerned about his faith. The Angel Gabriel called him from the sky.
"You have been chosen to receive the words of Allah," said the voice.
And thus Muhammad learned the verses of Quran, sent from on high.

The anniversary of that special time falls in the month of Ramadan.
So Muslims sacrifice as we've been bidden by our holy book, Quran.

Stuck Toast and Mud Pies

WE CELEBRATE KWANZAA

An African-American Celebration
From December 26 to January 1

The Ceremony:
Come. Join the family round a straw mat on the floor.
Place seven candles in a holder, not one more.
Add ears of corn, one for each child that we adore.
Pour water in a cup to toast our ancestors of yore.
Add fruit and seeds and gifts of creativity galore.

Now hang the Kwanzaa flag so that it faces east,
Then dance and laugh and sing and have a joyous feast.

The Meaning:
The seven candles, green, and black, and brilliant red
Stand for rich land, Black people, and the blood we've shed.

We honor self, our culture, our community,
And pass the cup to symbolize our unity.

We make a solemn pledge to use both heart and mind
To make a better world for all of humankind.

SCIENCE: NO HOMEWORK REQUIRED

This section has been reviewed for scientific accuracy by Richard A. Croley, Ph.D., and Manager of Intellectual Property and Patent Administration for the University of North Texas in Denton, Texas.

STUCK TOAST

It never fails; it's just my luck,
To have my piece of toast get stuck.
But toasters must be used with care
Because there's danger lurking there.

If you forget and poke about
With metal forks, there's little doubt
Electric charges, seeking ground,
Will toast YOU till you're nicely browned.

So, when you want that stubborn slice
That's stuck, remember this advice:
To help your piece of toast eject,
First pull the plug and disconnect.

TO SEE A RAINBOW

When the rainstorm turns to drizzle
And the sun starts poking through,
When black clouds go sweeping westward
And pale patches turn to blue,
Then it's time to watch for rainbows
Arching wide across the sky
Like a line of pastel laundry
Hung outside to slowly dry.

Now, you'll never see a rainbow
If you're facing toward the sun.
And it does no good to chase them
For you'll always be outrun.
Wealth is there as legends promise
In the beauty we behold
When the raindrops bend the sunlight
Into violet and gold.

Stuck Toast and Mud Pies

GOOD OLD GRAVITY

No matter how I try
To keep my ball high in the sky,
It won't stay up and I know why!

It's gravity that keeps things here on earth.
Without its force the entire human race,
And everything we own, would fall right off
And spin out into space...without a trace.

Our pods and tablets, cells and flat TVs
Would simply fly away and disappear.
Our scientists would race against the clock,
Inventing sticky stuff to keep us here.

Be thankful gravity
Not sticky stuff
Keeps you and me
Right here in place
Where we
Would much, much
Rather be.

SEEDS LEAVE HOME

A seed contains an embryo
Where roots and stems are growing,
With food stored up to nourish it
Till it gets where it's going.

If seeds kept dropping underneath
Their parent plant forever,
They'd never spread their seeds afar
So seeds are very clever.

They fly, they flutter, pop and glide,
Resort to aviation.
They prick, they stick, they hitch a ride
To spread through propagation.

Some plants that grow on river banks
Have seedlings made for floating.
They sail downstream where they can sprout
The embryo they're toting.

The dandelion makes seeds with fluff
That gives them elevation
So gentle winds can whisk them off
To start their new creation.

60   Stuck Toast and Mud Pies

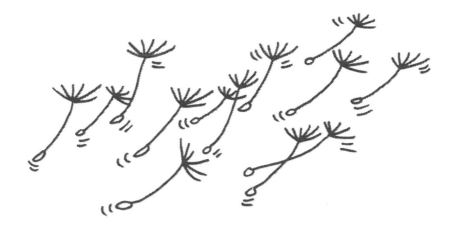

Don't be put off by touch-me-nots,
Their name is worth ignoring.
So touch their dried up pods, it's fun,
And POP, the seeds go soaring.

The seeds of maple, ash, and elm
Have wings with one end fatter.
When they spin down, the extra weight
Is what helps them to scatter.

The beggar stick has spines and barbs
That hitchhike on our clothing.
When we sit down to pick them off,
They grow where we've been roving.

Quick squirrels carry acorns off.
They drop some as they wander.
The acorn grows a mighty oak
Not where it fell, but yonder.

So, unlike us, when seeds leave home
They're really quite cold-hearted.
They never miss their moms and dads
Or cry, once they've departed.

EXPLAINING THUNDERSTORMS

A thunderstorm can be explained
With great sim-pli-ci-ty:
A lightning bolt is nothing more
Than e-lec-tri-ci-ty
That zigs about between the clouds
Or zags from clouds to ground.
Air zooms into the empty space
And BOOM...the thunder sound.

But when the clouds pile high and black
And thunder sounds horrific,
There's one way to explain the noise
That's not so scientific.
When lightning streaks across the sky
In dazzling demonstration,
Perhaps the clouds are clapping hands
To show appreciation.

Stuck Toast and Mud Pies

DEEP, DEEP DOWN DISCOVERY

Mid-ocean Ridge at the Galapagos, 1977

In the deepest dark depths of the ocean,
Down where sunlight can't reach to its floor,
Oceanographers thought nothing lived there,
But they don't think like that anymore.

A submersible craft they named Alvin*
Took them deep where no human could dive,
And they all were in awe to discover
There were millions of things there—alive.

Near warm springs their lights shone upon sponges,
On crustaceans and sluggish worms, too;
Giant mussels and tall spindly corals,
And on lice just as big as a shoe.

Shrimp were feeding near vents of volcanoes;
Starfish flourished where green plants can't grow.
We learned life down there didn't need sunlight;
They used energy formed down below.

* Named to honor the prime mover and crea-
tive inspiration for the vehicle, Allyn Vine.

A PRICELESS GIFT

There's a priceless natural resource—
    Millionaires can't match its worth.
It's a solid, gas, or liquid,
    That gives life to things on earth.

Each small molecule keeps moving,
    In its solid state it slows.
It moves freely when it's liquid,
    When it's gas, POOF! Off it goes.

When Jack Frost arrives to nip us
    And most other things contract
This clear substance starts expanding…
    A peculiar way to act.

All the clues have been presented.
    Have you guessed yet? Do you know?
That the priceless gift is water—
    Drink some down. It's H_2O.

Stuck Toast and Mud Pies

OIL AND WATER

The molecules of oil and water
   Do not mix.
It's hard to tell which one
   Is more contrary.
We shake and shake the salad dressing
   Up and down
And still their blending
   Is just temporary.

But when their stubbornness creates
   A magic glaze
Of iridescent purples, golden bronze,
   And vibrant blues
On top of roadside puddles,
   We are glad
Two elements—like oil and water—
   Simply hate to fuse.

TO THE MOON

President John F. Kennedy's Dream, 1961

John Kennedy declared that we would reach the moon;
To many it was just a distant dream.
The moon's uneven surface has no atmosphere;
Its temperature can swing to each extreme.

The distance to the only surface facing us:
More than two hundred thousand miles away.
To go so far, not knowing all that waited there,
Was dangerous. Some warned we should delay.

A Dream Realized, 1969

With Armstrong, Aldrin, and Collins now aboard
Apollo blasted off with mighty boom.
And once they went beyond the gravity of earth,
Columbia took them zooming toward the moon.

Up close, the moon became an awesome sight…
No longer slightly mottled, flat and pale.
The sun, reflecting on it from the earth,
Defined its seas and craters sharply in detail.

In spite of all the dangers that they bravely faced,
The astronauts* returned, and they were pleased
To show us pieces of the moon as proof
It's made of rock and dust; it's NOT made of green cheese.

The Astronauts:
Neal A. Armstrong, Mission Commander
Edwin E. "Buzz" Aldrin, Lunar Module Pilot
Michael "Mike" Collins, Command Module Pilot

WEIRD ONES

THEY HOP, THEY ROAR,
THEY ARE NO MORE.

THE ODORZEE

The problem with the Odorzee
Is its bazaar anatomy.
This beast is born with two left feet.
It can't advance. It can't retreat.
It stands there, helpless, day by day,
Just hoping that some hapless prey
Will wander by, so it can snatch
A tasty, belly-filling catch.

But Odorzees don't wash. They stink!
So, when their prey is on the brink
Of being caught, they sniff their foe.
They hold their noses. Off they go!

Poor Odorzee can never feast
Which, sadly, dooms this smelly beast.

THE DOILY KARTS

The feeble-minded Doily Karts
Could separate, like puzzle parts.
They parked their heads up in a tree
To keep watch on their enemy.

In nearby pools they soaked their feet
To get relief from summer heat,
While abdomen and tail would play
With friends that wandered by that day.

We must admire their special skill,
Which worked fine for this beast, until
They had to fight against their foes
By reconnecting head to toes.

Now this sad beast is history.
It failed the acid test. You see,
The feeble-minded Doily Karts
Forgot where they had left their parts.

Stuck Toast and Mud Pies

THE TINGY TONGUE-EE

The Tingy Tongue-ee male is mean.
He's never nice, or in-between.
If he can't get his way he's bound
To bellow, spit, and claw the ground.
Just like a misbehaving child
He stamps his feet when he is riled.

He sticks his tongue out at his mate
Then realizes, much too late,
In anger he forgot this fact:
Once his tongue's out, it won't retract!

Now he can never eat his food...
Which serves him right for being rude.

THE TWEEDLE DEEDLE

The Tweedle Deedle
      Flies so fast
It's never here...
      It's always past.

So once it's left
      Its neighborhood
The Tweedle Deedle's
      Gone for good.

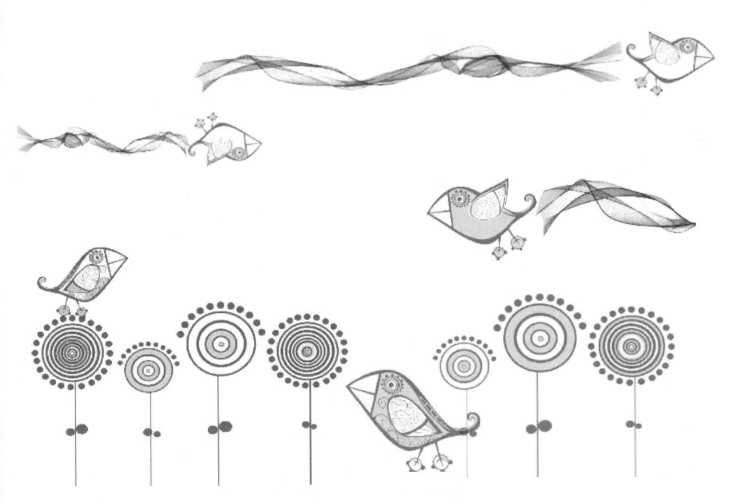

THE GOOF-OFF BIRD

The Goof-Off bird won't be here long.
So listen for its lazy song.

    This slugabed
        Hates exercise.
    It loves to loaf;
        It never flies.
    It will not peck;
        It will not scratch.
    Its sleepy eggs
        Refuse to hatch.
    It much prefers
        To take its rest
    Than build itself
        A proper nest.
    Goof-Off is never
        In the mood
    To make an effort
        To catch food.

This bird must change its ways real fast
Or its next breath may be its last.

Stuck Toast and Mud Pies

THE SHRINKING VYLET

The Shrinking Vylet's very shy
Especially when some passers-by
Out walking on a sunny day
Decide they'd like a nice bouquet.

To hide itself from probing eyes,
Each time it shrinks to half its size.
Now, having shrunk itself so small,
The Vylet's hardly here at all.

Weird Ones

THE PLUTO FLY TRAPS

The Pluto Fly Traps, like their kin,
Ate flying bugs they trapped within.
Until the leader of their clan
Became a vegetarian!

"A meatless meal is best," it said.
"Stop eating bugs. Eat plants instead."

This proved to be a handicap
Since plants did not fall in their trap.
The nearby plants refused to fly...
So kiss this foolish plant goodbye.

THE SUCTION SNOUT

The Suction Snout swims through the weeds.
It's clocked at supersonic speeds.
But when a boat gets in its way
(Which happens nearly every day)
Its tiny brain works much too slow
To signal STOP! It's still on GO!

Full speed ahead, its suction cup
Hits hard, and Suction Snout is stuck.
It wiggles, thrashes all about
But cannot loosen up its snout.
If it's not freed without delay
The Suction Snout lives just one day.

THE VAMPIRE YUCKS

The Vampire Yucks
Exist on blood.
It's sad to hear them
Moan and groan.
They're dying off
In droves because
The blood they're sucking
Is their own.

THE VITA-GROW

The Vita-Grow will never see
The ripe old age of two or three.

This spindly creature grows so fast
In just one week its head is past
The treetops, and it's reached so high
It's up where terns and eagles fly.

Its growing is still incomplete
When it has reached ten thousand feet.
Into the stratosphere it grows
Where jets go zooming past its nose.

But there the air is thin, and so
The Vita-Grow gets vertigo!
It teeters, wobbles, falls, and then
It can't get to its feet again.

And so it comes as no surprise
That soon we'll see this beast's demise.

THE INSIDE OUTER

The Inside Outer once was feared.
It's now considered simply weird.
Its hide's inside, its organs out,
So heart and stomach flap about.

When lice and fleas and vermin hatch,
There's no way this poor beast can scratch.

The food it swallows cannot find
The stomach, so, though it has dined
On rutabagas, corn, and hay,
The Inside Outer wastes away.

THE ROADWAY WILLET

The Roadway Willet prowled at night;
With sticky feet it caught its prey.
But when car headlights come in sight
It could not quickly run away.

Poor Roadway's feet stayed stuck like glue
Though horns were honked and brakes applied.
So bid this beast a sad adieu.
Alas, that's how this species died.

Stuck Toast and Mud Pies

THE STUMBLE BOING!

The Stumble Boing!
    You doubtless know,
Has one small foot
    With one big toe.
When running fast
    To catch its prey,
That giant toe
    Gets in the way.
And so it trips
    And hits its head...

Within a week...
    It's
        Always
            Dead.

THE BRATTY-WAY

The offspring of the Bratty-Way
Are naughty. They will not obey.

Their manners are deplorable.
They jabber while their mouths are full.
They drool, they gobble, slobber, slurp
And when their meal is done, they burp!

When father gives his cubs a whack
They make a face behind his back.

They're taught to stay, not wander far
Into the woods where Woozies are.
Although their mothers tell them NO!
That's just exactly where they go.

And so this disobedient bunch
Becomes the Woozies' favorite lunch.

THE STUPID STICKLY

The Stupid Stickly plants are weeds
Which multiply by spreading seeds
With long and pointy, sticky spines
That open where the bright sun shines.

These spines are meant to hitch their rides
On animals with shaggy hides,
Then drop and flourish in the earth
Some distance from their place of birth.

Instead, this weed picks specimens
That sleep all day in darkened dens.
And soon, without their dose of light,
Their seeds develop cruddy blight.

Alas, they'll learn, but much too late,
They will no longer propagate.

Stuck Toast and Mud Pies

THE WILD GANEW

Deep in a grove of tall bamboo
There once lived herds of Wild Ganew.
They had gigantic tails and paws
With nasty curved and pointy claws.
They ate smooth Finkles by the score,
But they don't eat them any more.

The Finkles schemed, then each one grew
A beard, which tickled the Ganew
So much they giggled, lost their breath,
And simply laughed themselves to death.

THE DUH DUH BIRD

The Duh Duh birds were ding-a-lings.
They flapped their legs and walked on wings.
No early birds, they slept till noon.
The songs they sang were out of tune.

They hatched no Duh Duh birds, for they'd
Eat every single egg they laid.

They pecked their friends and preened their prey.
I ask you, is that any way
To multiply when acting weird?
Of course not, so they disappeared.

Weird Ones

ONCE UPON A POEM

THE REMARKABLE BUBBLES OF MARY LEE HUBBLES

This is the story of Mary Lee Hubbles
   And the strange things that happened
      Because she blew bubbles.

When Mary was just a wee babe in her crib
Mother covered her up with a giant-size bib,
   For the bubbles she blew,
      As she'd babble and coo,
         Would envelop her nose
           And her tummy and toes,
             Flowing over her bed
               And her pink flowered spread,
Until even her teddy lay hidden from view
By showers of bubbles that Mary Lee blew.

When Mary Lee learned how to drink from a cup,
She blew in her milk till it bubbled right up.
   It brimmed over the top,
      It poured onto the floor.
         Mary giggled and gurgled
           And bubbled some more,
For bubbles were what Mary most loved to see,
Until Mother, announced, "That's enough, Mary Lee!"

As she grew, bubble baths were a glorious thrill.
Mary splashed and made mountains of bubbles until
   Bubbles flowed from the house
      Like a thick, foamy cloud
         Streaming into the street
           Where the cop on the beat
             Blew, "tweet-tweet," on his whistle
             To hold back the crowd.
When the clamor died down, Mother solemnly vowed,
"That's your last bubble bath; it's no longer allowed."

On a visit, her aunt brought her soap-bubble stuff
With a soap-bubble pipe to dip in and to puff.
      Soapy bubbles went floating,
          Caught up by the breeze,
              Onto fences and bushes and
                  Wires and trees.
The birds, who were chirping and peacefully perching,
Started skidding and sliding and swaying and lurching.

And suddenly, PLOP! falling down from above,
      Slipped five scolding jays,
          Four larks and a dove.
              Six wobbly warblers came tumbling, then
              Two robins, six sparrows,
                  And one baby wren.
Mother cried, "Mary Lee, please attend to my words:
No more soap-bubble stuff, for it's raining down birds."

Stuck Toast and Mud Pies

One day, chewing gum (with a sniffily cold),
Mary coughed and ker-chooed a big sneeze, and behold!
      The gum on the tips
          Of her rosy red lips
             Blew outward and bubbled
               And tripled in size,
                   Then, BOOM! it exploded
                     Right into her eyes.
Mother threw up her hands and declared in despair,
"Gracious me, Mary Lee, you have gum in your hair!"

Now the damage was done, for the minute she knew
She could blow giant bubbles, she blew and she blew.
      And there wasn't a place,
          Not a book or a lamp
             Or a chair or a vase,
               That didn't show traces
                   Of Mary Lee's chewing.
Father said, "Mary Lee, I see trouble a-brewing.
I'm afraid bubble blowing will be your undoing."

When Mary Lee started to school in the fall,
Her teacher said, "Gum's not permitted at all."
      But Mary adored
          Chewing bubble gum so,
             She wadded it up
               And, so no one would know,
                   Tucked it under her tongue,
                     And tried hard not to blow.
But somehow the bubble gum urge got so strong
(Though she knew it was terribly, terribly wrong),
She bent down and pretended
      To tie up her shoe,
          Then she quietly blew
             A wee bubble or two.
The teacher said, "Mary, we see what you're doing.
You get fifteen detentions for bubble gum chewing."

Mary's parents grew worried about her condition.
So they whisked Mary off to her pediatrician.
  Dr. Hill said, "Say ah."
    Dr. Hill checked her heart,
      Her knees and her nostrils
        And each other part.
  Reading medical books
    And consulting with others,
      With teachers and doctors
        And fathers and mothers,
Dr. Hill sadly stated, "The outlook is poor.
Mary cannot stop chewing. There's simply no cure."

Although Mary was sweet, never sassy or bold,
Though she did all her chores, the sad truth must be told.
  Mary spent her allowance
    On bubble gum balls,
      Dropping gum wads about
        In the streets and the malls,
  Till the people in town
    Stuck to sidewalks and floors,
      To benches, to bleachers,
        To counters in stores.
Not even the swings and the seesaws were spared.
"Mary Lee must be stopped!" the townspeople declared.

Late that night a reporter announced on the news,
"Lightfoot Larry, the thief, wearing soft ballet shoes,
  Is stealing from shops
    All the cash he can carry.
  He has robbed seven doctors
    Their patients and nurses,
      Made off with their wallets,
        Their watches and purses.
He has pilfered from homes, stuffing big pillow cases
With silver and jewels, and leaving no traces."

Stuck Toast and Mud Pies

People cried in alarm, "Mary's problem can wait.
We must catch Lightfoot Larry before it's too late."
They gathered together and formed a committee,
Painted slogans on signs that said, "SAVE OUR FINE CITY".
       They marched and protested
           In front of the jail.
              "We want Larry arrested
                  And held without bail!"
Said the sheriff, "I'm sorry, we've tried to pursue,
But Larry's so clever, we can't find a clue."

Then one day Mary went to the bank with her mother.
They waited in line, one in back of the other.
       Mary Lee was, of course,
         Chewing bubble gum gaily—
           A thing that she did not just weekly,
             But daily—
When the man right in front
        (Whom she happened to hear),
          In a low, snarly voice,
             Whispered to the cashier,
"You have nothing to fear, don't act foolish or funny,
Do not sound the alarm, just hand over your money."

Lightfoot Larry! thought Mary. *Oh, what can I do*?
But although she felt frightened, she suddenly knew.
       Blowing giant-size globules
        Of bubble gum goo,
          She enclosed Larry's head
           In a rubbery glue.

Bubbles covered his hair,
    Bushy eyebrows and nose,
        Bubbles flowed down his chin,
            Covered all of his clothes.
Bubbles circled his socks,
    Slithered onto his shoes,
        Which got glued to the floor
            With bubble gum ooze.
"You've got bubbles all over that man!" Mom complained.
"I've caught Larry, the crook!" Mary proudly explained.

The squad cars arrived with a screech and a wail,
Loosened up Lightfoot Larry, and rushed him to jail.

The judge found him guilty and sent him away
To the state penitentiary for life, plus one day.

When the townspeople heard the good news, they were thrilled.
They poured out of their homes till the streets were all filled.
    "Hurray!" said the mayor,
        "For Mary Lee Hubbles.
            She has rescued our town
                Blowing chewing gum bubbles!
No more will that crook
    Rob our stores and our banks.
        We must figure a way to show
            Mary our thanks."
So a statue of Mary was built in the square
With a crown of bronze bubbles adorning her hair.

All the village took part in a great celebration,
Giving Mary Lee Hubbles a standing ovation.

Mary spoke to the crowd, and she solemnly swore,
"Though I love to chew gum, I will litter no more."

Mayor Green said, "Dear Mary, you've ended our troubles.
Here's a gift from the town, so you'll always blow bubbles."
Mary Lee was impressed,
(Have you already guessed?)
With the life-long supply
Of the gum she loved best,
And to hold it, the world's largest gumball machine
Inscribed, "Mary Lee Hubbles, Our Bubble Gum Queen."

Stuck Toast and Mud Pies

THE QUESTIONMARK TWINS

The Questionmark Twins are a curious pair.
They ask HOW? They ask WHO? They ask WHAT? WHY and WHERE?

"Why does the rain fall? And what makes the dew?
And why does the day start when nighttime is through?"

"I'll ask Mother," said Sam. "No, it's my turn," said Pam.
"I thought of it first, so I'm asking, I am."

But Mother was phoning a real estate client.
"Not now…and besides, you should be self-reliant."

"How big is the sky, and what makes it so blue?
Why doesn't it fall? Is it held up with glue?"

"I'll ask Father," said Pam. "No, it's my turn," said Sam.
"I thought of it first, so I'm asking, I am."

But over the roar of the car's carburetor
Father yelled, "I can't hear you. I'll talk to you later."

"Why does a dog like to chase balls and sticks,
And wear smelly collars to stop fleas and ticks?"

"I'll ask Rover," said Sam. "No, it's my turn," said Pam.
"I thought of it first, so I'm asking, I am."

But Rover woofed once and returned to his bone.
The Twins said, "He's hungry, we'll leave him alone."

"Why does a cat always land on its feet?
And who taught the kittens to keep themselves neat?"

"I'll ask Fluffy," said Pam. "No, it's my turn," said Sam.
"I thought of it first, so I'm asking, I am."

But Fluffy replied with a mew and a purr
And went back to washing her whiskers and fur.

At breakfast Pam asked, "What makes cereal pop?
And when it gets soggy what makes the pop stop?"

"I'll ask Grandma," said Sam. "No it's my turn," said Pam.
"I thought of it first, so I'm asking, I am."

But Grandma said, "Hurry, you'll be late for school.
Brush your teeth when you finish…you both know the rule."

"Who decided the color a school bus should be?
Is yellow a color that's easy to see?"

"I'll ask Harry, said Pam. "No, it's my turn," said Sam.
"I thought of it first, so I'm asking, I am."

But the bus kids were loud, Harry's face turned bright red.
"Ask your teacher at school," he impatiently said.

"How high are the Andes, and where is Peru?
And why do some camels have one hump, not two?"

"I'll ask Teacher," said Sam. "No, it's my turn," said Pam.
"I thought of it first, so I'm asking, I am."

But Miss Jones said, "I'm sorry, it's time to start class.
I can't answer you now. Here's a Media pass."

Stuck Toast and Mud Pies

So Pam and Sam went to the Media Center.
And a sign on the door told them...

```
WELCOME
PLEASE ENTER
```

The Center had books and
Devices galore.
Pam and Sam used them all,
They searched links by the score.

They learned all about mountains,
Cats and dogs; rain and dew;
Why our cereal pops,
And the sky appears blue.

So the Questionmark Twins
Proudly said, "From the start,
We'll find answers ourselves.
That's the way to get smart."

Once Upon a Poem

FACES

Look at each face and here is what you see:
    A nose,
        Two eyes,
            Two lips, a chin,
    Eyebrows and lashes,
        Teeth and ears,
            And hair and skin.
If all the parts of faces are the same,
How do we learn to give each face its special name?

We all have hair, BUT...
    There's blond, brunette, red, white, and gray.
    Some wear it flat, or spiked with spray.
    Hair curls or waves or limply hangs.
    It's braided, bobbed or cut with bangs.

    Some men don't like to shave, and so
    Their face is where they let hair grow.

We all have eyebrows, BUT...
    Some brows behave and stay in place.
    Some straggle all across the face.
    Brows arch up high to show surprise.
    Frowns squeeze brows tight across the eyes.

Stuck Toast and Mud Pies

We all have eyes, BUT...
>Some eyes are blue, some kitten gray.
>Shy eyes gaze down or glance away.
>Rough, angry eyes look mean and cold.
>Dark brown eyes glow with flecks of gold.
>
>Sad, teary eyes say, "I feel hurt."
>Bold, saucy eyes will tease and flirt.

We all have lashes, BUT...
>Black lashes make a clear, dark row.
>The red and blond ones barely show.
>Some curl, some grow straight as a stick.
>Mascara makes some dark and thick.

We all have noses, BUT...
>Some run and drip, some itch and wheeze.
>They're narrow, broad, turn red and sneeze.
>Some tilt so high that they expose
>The nostrils underneath the nose.
>
>Some hook or hump, some twist, some droop;
>For them it's hard to eat their soup!

We all have lips, BUT...
　　Some purse and pucker, peck or pout.
　　Some lips are full and stick far out.
　　Some make a line and stretch out thin.
　　Some lips curl up to make a grin.

We all have teeth, BUT...
　　Some teeth grow in their proper place.
　　For crooked ones we wear a brace.
　　When second ones are growing in
　　Kids smile a jack-o'-lantern grin.

　　If we don't brush them as we're told,
　　They're drilled, then filled with white or gold.

We all have chins, BUT...
　　Some chins jut forward, bold and strong.
　　Some chins are short, some extra-long.
　　Some people grow two chins or three
　　When they eat everything they see.

We all have ears, BUT...
　　Some ears lie close against the head.
　　Some flap out in the breeze instead.
　　Some lobes have holes for wearing rings,
　　Large hoops or giant dish-like things.

　　Some ears blush red, some grow long hairs.
　　Some people even wiggle theirs.

Stuck Toast and Mud Pies

We all have skin, BUT...
        Some skin has freckles, moles or pimples,
        Wrinkles, warts, or dents and dimples.
        Our colors go from dark to light.
        Some skin hangs loose, some hugs us tight.

And so, though face parts are the same,
        Each face looks different, too.
That's how you know
        Who others are
And how we know you're YOU!

BIG WORDS ABOUT ME
FROM A TO Z

Aa I'm AFFABLE

    I'm friendly, so I share
    My toys and treats,
    And I play fair.

Bb I'm BEWILDERED

    When there's something I can't do,
    Like counting to a million,
    Or tying up my shoe.

Cc I'm CANTANKEROUS

    Don't want to go to bed,
    I'm tired and I'm cross.
    But Mom just tucks me in
    And reminds me she's the boss.

Dd I'm DEXTEROUS

    My hands can push
        A skinny thread
            Into a needle's eye,
  Or pile my blocks
        Above my head
            Away up high.

Stuck Toast and Mud Pies

Ee   **I'm ENTERPRISING**

           If it's rainy
                Or I have to play alone,
           I create imaginary kingdoms
                All my own.

Ff   **I'm FORLORN**

           When my new puppy runs away,
           Or my best friend is sick
           And can't come out to play.

Gg   **I'm GREGARIOUS**

           When new kids move nearby
           I go right up and smile, and say,
           A cheery, "Hi!"

Hh   **I'm HYGIENIC**

           I wash my hands
                Before I eat.
           I brush my teeth
                And keep my body
                    Clean and neat.

Ii   **I'm IMPECCABLE**

           A neat-freak,
           Keep my room clean,
           Smooth the spread.

           No junk's in view…as long as you
           Don't peek beneath my bed.

Dictionary meanings
of these words, along
with a pronunciation
guide, can be found
on pages 106 through
108.

Jj   I'm JOVIAL

  I laugh, do funny things,
        Make other people smile.
  A super sense of humor…
        That's my style.

Kk   I'm KINETIC

  Energetic,
  I'm in motion every minute.
  Up and down and round and round
  Like a top whirls when you spin it.

Ll   I'm LOQUACIOUS

  I like to talk a lot.
  If you're like me,
  A wagging tongue is what you've got.

Mm   I'm MATHEMATICAL

  I know two quarters
  Plus two more make four.
  Now, double that to eight,
  To make a dollar more.

Nn   I'm NIMBLE

  I can twist my body,
        Then unwind.
  And great ideas come tumbling from
        My agile mind.

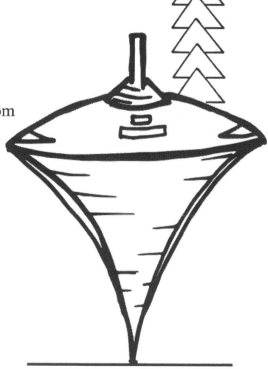

104   Stuck Toast and Mud Pies

Oo   I'm OBSERVANT

> Notice everything
> Down to the last detail,
> From an astronaut in orbit
> To a tiny ocean snail.

Pp   I'm PATRIOTIC

> I shiver with delight
> > When, on July the Fourth,
> Exploding rockets fling their colored stars
> > Into the night.

Qq   I'm QUIESCENT

> When, at times,
> I lose my hustle.
> I am quiet, calm and still…
> Don't move a muscle.

Rr   I'm RHYTHMIC

> I was born to dance.
> I polka when I get the chance.
> I break-dance, swing and do-si-do.
>
> Oops, sorry…did I mash your toe?

Ss　　I'm SPONTANEOUS

　　　　I do things suddenly.
　　　　I bellow in the shower,
　　　　　　Or pick my mom a flower.

　　　　It surprises even me
　　　　When I do things
　　　　So unexpectedly.

Tt　　I'm THRIFTY

　　　　Careful money-wise.
　　　　I save each penny, and surprise!
　　　　My pennies grow
　　　　　　…and grow
　　　　　　　　…and grow
　　　　To many, many, many.

Uu　　I'm UBIQUITOUS

　　　　You'll see me everywhere,
　　　　At school or at a country fair.
　　　　Go view the monkeys at the zoo
　　　　Then look around…I'll be there too.

Vv　　I'm VORACIOUS

　　　　When it's mealtime
　　　　　　I'm as hungry as a beast.
　　　　　　　And though salad is delightful,
　　　　　　　Vitamins in every bite full,
　　　　It's on pizza that I really
　　　　Love to feast.

Ww   I'm WHIMSICAL

        I'm prankish, I'm kooky or mean.
        But there's nothing to fear,
              On just one day a year,
        I yell, "Boo! Happy Halloween!"

Xx   I'm XENOPHILIC

        Love to learn and understand
        About the ways of people
        From a foreign land.

Yy   I'm YEOMANLY

        A coward I am not.
        I act bravely
        Even when I get a shot.

Zz   I'm ZEALOUS

        An eager go-getter
        No matter what my goal;
              Clarinet-er
                    Internet-er,
                          Pirouette-er
                            I aim to do it better.

BIG WORDS DICTIONARY

Key to Pronunciation Marks:
The ə is pronounced like the a in about.
A line above a vowel (ā, ē, ī, ō, ū) means it says its name as in fāce, ēat, īce, ōnly, or mūsic.
The (ˈ) tells which part of the word is accented or stressed.

AFFABLE:
Adjective: \ˈa-fə-bəl\; I am pleasant and friendly. I like to be around people.

BEWILDERED:
Transitive verb, past tense: \bi-ˈwil-dərd, also bē-\; I am puzzled and confused by some things that are hard to do or to understand.

CANTANKEROUS:
Adjective: \kan-ˈtaŋ-k(ə)-rəs\; I act crabby and quarrelsome once in a while.

DEXTEROUS:
Adjective: \ˈdek-st(ə-)rəs\; My hands and fingers work well together to do a hard job.

ENTERPRISING:
Adjective: \ ˈent-ə(r)-prī-ziŋ\; I start things on my own; I am always ready to try something new.

FORLORN:
Adjective: \fər-ˈlȯrn\; When bad things happen, I sometimes feel miserable, sad or alone.

GREGARIOUS:
Adjective: \gri-ˈger-ē-əs\; I make friends easily. I enjoy being with other people.

HYGIENIC:
Adjective: \hī-ˈjē-nik\; I like to be clean and healthy. I hate germs.

IMPECCABLE:
Adjective: \()im-ˈpek-ə-bəl\; I like things to be neat and in their places. I'm fussy about how I look.

JOVIAL:

Adjective: \ˈjō-vē-əl, also vyəl\; I am full of fun and get-up-and-go. I love to tell jokes.

KINETIC:
Adjective: \kə-ˈne-tik, or kī-\; I am very active. Sitting still is very hard. I wiggle a lot.

LOQUACIOUS:
Adjective: \lō-ˈkwā-shəs\; I talk, talk, talk. Sometimes at school I get into trouble for talking too much.

MATHEMATICAL:
Adjective: \ˌmath-ˈma-ti-kəl, also ma-thə-\; I understand how numbers work. I can add and subtract big numbers.

NIMBLE:
Adjective: \ˈnim-bəl\; I am able to move my body quickly. My mind works fast, too.

OBSERVANT:
Adjective: \- əbˈzər-vənt \; I watch and listen carefully. I pay attention when I look at something, then I remember all about it.

PATRIOTIC:
Adjective: \ˌpā-trē-ˈä-tik\; I love my country. One way I show I care about our country is by picking up my trash.

QUIESCENT:
Adjective: \kwē-ˈes-ənt\; I can be very quiet sometimes. At those times, I don't cause much trouble.

RHYTHMIC:
Adjective: \ˈrith-mik\; I love the beat of music. I can't help moving and tapping my feet when the band is playing.

SPONTANEOUS:
Adjective: \spän-ˈtā-nē-əs\; Sometimes I do things without planning to, like kissing grandma when she doesn't even ask.

THRIFTY:
Adjective: \ˈthrif-tē\; I am careful about spending money or wasting things like paper or food. I save a part of my allowance each week.

UBIQUITOUS:
Adjective: \yü-'bi-kwə-təs\; I go here, there and everywhere. Friends say that wherever they go, I'm there, too.

VORACIOUS:
Adjective: \vȯ-'rā-shəs, also və-\; I am always hungry. My parents say I must have hollow legs because I eat so much.

WHIMSICAL:
Adjective: \'hwim-zi-kəl, also 'wim-\; I get a weird idea and suddenly do something silly or strange. I only mean it in fun, but sometimes I get into mischief.

XENOPHILIC:
Adjective: \zen-ō-'fil-ik\; I love meeting people from other countries. Someday I'll travel around the world and study the customs of other lands.

YEOMANLY:
Adjective: \'y ō –mən-lē\; I try to be brave when I am hurt or when things are difficult.

ZEALOUS
Adjective: \'ze-ləs\; I get excited about doing my favorite things. I put my whole heart into projects and activities that I love.

A CAT'S LIFE

My name is Putney. I'm a cat.
My tail is long, my body's fat.
My fur is black, my whiskers white.
I close my golden eyes up tight,
      And then I sleep.

My bowl says "Putney" so I see
Exactly where my food will be.
The boy who lives here fills my dish.
I eat my favorite—tuna fish!
      And then I sleep.

I jump on shelves and window sills.
I'm very careful. Nothing spills.
I like to find a quiet place
To clean my whiskers and my face,
      And then I sleep.

The girl who lives here brushes me.
I purr, contented as can be.
She rubs my ears and strokes my back
To help my fur stay shiny black,
      And then I sleep.

I jump up high to bat a ball.
I land on four feet—never fall.
I play with feathers, jingling toys,
I soon get tired of the noise,
      And then I sleep.

The people here do lots of chores
Like making beds and washing floors.
They dig a garden, sow some seeds.
I watch them pull up nasty weeds,
      And then I sleep.

I see a shape. What can it be?
Oh, no! It's coming after me.
It's huge and fierce with giant paws.
I tense my body, bare my claws.
My fur stands up. I switch my tail.
I arch my back. I hiss and wail,
      And then I LEAP!

                                               Stuck Toast and Mud Pies

But that mean beast had disappeared.
Where did it go, that thing I feared?
Alone again, I crouch down low
To rest, and suddenly I know.
The scary thing I saw was fine
Because that shadow shape was MINE.
        It's safe to sleep.

I circle round to make my bed.
I curl my paws beneath my head,
        And then I sleep.

Once Upon a Poem

MUD PIES

POEMS FOR YOUNG ONES

FIRST STEPS

I stand up tall.
Boom! Down I fall.

But I don't cry.
I try and try.

I stand again.
One step, and then

Two, three, and four,
Five, six, then more.

See what I did?
I'm one great kid.

BATH TIME

One, two,
In I go,
I get wet
From head to toe.

Three, four,
Rub-a-dub,
Chasing soap
Around the tub.

Five, six,
Duck and boat,
Having fun
With toys that float.

Seven, eight,
That was fun,
Drying off
And now I'm done.

Nine, ten,
Into bed,
Baths make me
A sleepy head.

Stuck Toast and Mud Pies

THE TICKLE GAME

(Adapted from a Danish game for babies)

Adult Reader: Take the baby's finger, using it to touch each part of its little face as you recite the poem. When you say the last line, tickle the baby under the chin.

Touch my head,
Touch my brow.
Close my eyes,
And open now.

Touch my nose,
Touch my lip.
Then...under my chin,
Go dika-dika-dik.

Babies usually laugh delightedly and want to play again.

The Danish words:
>Hoved (Head)
>Pande (Forehead)
>Øjesten (Eye)
>Naesetip (Nosetip)
>Mundelip (Lip)
>Hageflip (Chin)
>Dika-dika-dik (A made up word)

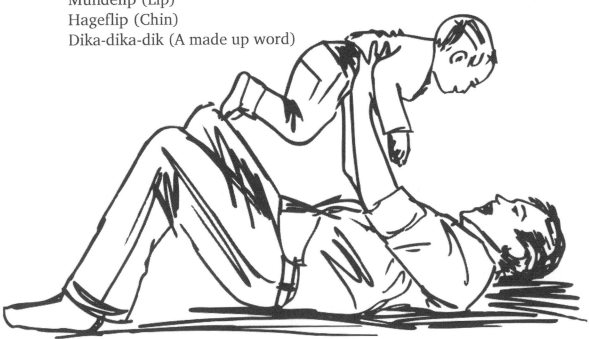

THE BARNYARD ZOO

Our mom and our dad and our grandparents, too,
Are taking us out to the barnyard zoo.

The line is so long, and we wiggle and wait,
Then Dad buys the tickets. We're through the gate.

A duck waddles by saying, "Quack, quack. Quack, quack."
Her fluffy young ducklings lined up at her back.

The newly born lambs stand on weak, wobbly feet.
We touch their thick wool and they softly bleat.

The patient cows wait, munching hay in their stalls.
When milking begins, they make mooing calls.

Stuck Toast and Mud Pies

In the corner a mouser laps up some cool milk.
We pet the cat's fur. It's as smooth as silk.

Grandma scatters dry corn on the henhouse ground
And dozens of chickens cluck and cackle around.

A mare and her foal slowly chomp on some oats.
We brush their long manes and their chestnut coats.

Grandpa calls, "See the momma pig there in her pen?
She's nursing her piglets. How many? Yes, ten."

Our favorite's the bunny. We cuddle it near.
We stroke its grey fur then it flicks its long ear.

The gates are now closing. We're sad the day ends
As we all wave goodbye to our new barnyard friends.

PIES, PIES, PIES

My mom makes lots of yummy pies.
We have one every night.
Hot apple, cherry, custard cream.
We gobble down each bite.

My friend and I make pies like Mom's.
We mix our dough. It's fun.
We roll them out and flatten them,
Then bake them in the sun.

We call our friends to come to tea
To share our special treat.
"No way," they say, "we won't taste those,
'Cause mud's not good to eat."

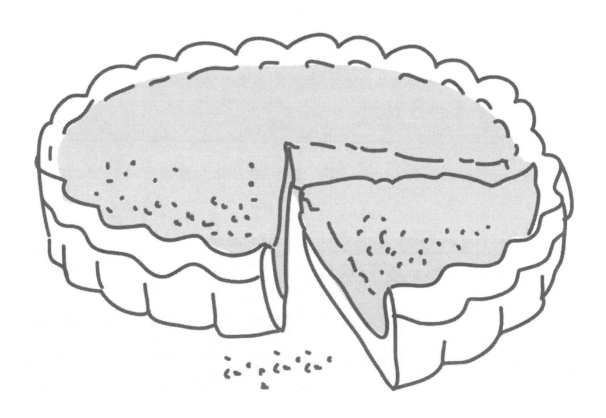

Stuck Toast and Mud Pies

LET'S PLAY PRETEND

It's pouring outside and we're stuck in the house.
We can play at pretend, be a dog or a mouse.

Or we'll chug up a hill and "Choo! Choo!" like a train.
Spread our arms open wide and zoom by like a plane.

We'll raise a great tent using chairs and some sheets,
And go camping with bedrolls and chocolate treats.

Maybe pile giant blocks, make a grocery store;
Put some food on the racks and fling open the door.

The customers come and they buy from the shelves,
But some cereal's left, so we'll eat that ourselves.

We'll sail to an island with palm trees and sand,
Where we're crowned king and queen of the magical land.

Look, it's sunny again; we can go out to play.
But we'll save our pretends for the next rainy day.

I WONDER WHY

At night I gaze up at the sparkling Milky Way
And wonder where those stars go in the day.

Each wren or robin spreads its wings and quickly flies.
I flap my arms, but cannot soar the skies.

Young fish can dart and swim the moment they arrive.
Why do I belly flop each time I dive?

Some nights the moon is big; sometimes it's very small,
Yet on most days I seldom see the moon at all.

Why does a baby only crawl; why can't a baby talk?
While I can say big words and I can walk?

I wait along the shore until the sun has set.
When it sinks in the sea does it get wet?

My questions need some answers, and it would be fun
Dear Reader, if you tried to answer just this one...

The sky's the brightest, bluest blue I've ever seen,
But just this time, why can't it turn bright green?

Stuck Toast and Mud Pies

PEEKING AROUND

I peek out the window, and what do I see?
My father is planting a new apple tree.

I peek in my brother's room. What do I see?
He's NOT doing homework. He's watching TV.

Mom opens her pocketbook. What do I see?
A lipstick, a comb, and a bright shiny key.

I peek in my sister's room. What do I see?
She's playing with dolls, and she's serving them tea.

I peek in the doghouse, and what do I see?
Our puppy is scratching a big pesky flea.

I peek in a basket, and what do I see?
Our cat has had kittens, a litter of three.

I peek in the mirror, and what do I see?
The curious one in the family. Me!

FOOD SHOPPING WITH MOM

I love to go with mom to shop.
We take a cart, and in I hop.

I ride up high where I can spy
The things we need as I roll by.

I point out apples in their bins;
Bananas with bright yellow skins.

Big watermelons, striped with green,
Some strawberries, tucked in between.

We buy some eggs, some orange cheese,
A jug of milk, and frozen peas.

The cereals fill one whole row.
Into the cart my favorites go.

And since I helped my mom a lot
I get to eat the things we bought!

Stuck Toast and Mud Pies

A HARD DAY'S WORK

My mom and dad work hard, it's true,
But I am busy all day, too.

I comb my hair so it looks neat.
I wash my hands before I eat.

I clean my plate of all that's there.
I fold my napkin so it's square.

I run to catch a flying ball
Before it sails across the wall.

I kiss my baby sister's nose.
I count her fingers and her toes.

I feed our cat some tuna fish.
I pour fresh water in her dish.

Into the kitchen, down the hall
I march to music, straight and tall.

By night time I'm a sleepy head...
I've worked all day; it's time for bed.

Mud Pies

ACKNOWLEDGEMENTS

Over a span of many years, my writers group has patiently listened to and critiqued these poems and their many revisions. Though the group composition has varied, Carol H. Behrman, Elizabeth A. Conard, Joan Hiatt Harlow, Gail E. Hedrick, Diane Robertson and Elizabeth Wall, all published writers, all insightful, intelligent women, have celebrated one another's successes. I cannot thank them enough for their invaluable help and support.

My daughter, Ann, is my loyal fan and honest critic. She makes sure that I reword and rephrase until my meaning is clear. She suggests new paths and challenging tangents to follow. I so appreciate her caring and her razor sharp mind. I'm also grateful to her husband, Rick Croley, Ph.D, for checking the accuracy of the science poems and for teaching me how one spot in the ocean can be so vastly different from another.

Special thanks go to my back-up groups: my dear family; my NOW friends; my Friday and Thursday Friends; my Connecticut Friends; and my great Sarasota neighbors. They all hold a place in my heart; they keep me learning, laughing and loving.

Finally, thanks to Eric Wyatt of Words Matter for keeping my stress level in low gear. I sincerely appreciate his detailed answers to zillions of questions, and his patient guidance in getting this book to market.

Stuck Toast and Mud Pies

CONTRIBUTING ARTISTS

Rik Vasquez is a digital artist specializing in storyboards, graphic novel art, and book illustrations. When not drawing, he spends time finger painting plastic dinosaur toys with his 3 year old daughter. Rik's art portfolio can be found online at www.storysketcher.com.

Lauren Dahlhauser is a third year photojournalism major at Ball State University who is passionate about creating many forms of art. She runs a small photography business on the side: Lauren Dahlhauser Photography (www.laurendahlhauserphotography.com). Lauren specializes in natural light portrait and lifestyle photography. Email: laurenphotog211@gmail.com

Jaime Bell is a digital artist whose special creatures grace the Weird Ones section of this book. She is 23 years old and lives in New Jersey. Jamie can be contacted at JamieB04@hotmail.com.

Zach Bretz is a third year Visual Communications major at Ball State University who is passionate about the fine arts and creating his own work as well. He is currently working on creating a wide range portfolio for when he graduates. Zach can be contacted at ztbretzdesign@gmail.com

INDEX

Made in the USA
Middletown, DE
30 August 2017